Post-Traumatic Stress Disorder

The GOSPEL for REAL LIFE series

Abuse: Finding Hope in Christ

Anxiety: Anatomy and Cure

Borderline Personality: A Scriptural Perspective

Burnout: Resting in God's Fairness

Cutting: A Healing Response

Depression: The Sun Always Rises

God's Attributes: Rest for Life's Struggles

Post-Traumatic Stress Disorder: Recovering Hope

Sexual Abuse: Beauty for Ashes

Vulnerability: Blessing in the Beatitudes

Brad Hambrick, Series Editor

Post-Traumatic Stress Disorder

RECOVERING HOPE

JEREMY LELEK

P&R
PUBLISHING
P.O. BOX 817 • PHILLIPSBURG • NEW JERSEY 08865-0817

ISBN: 978-1-59638-421-7 (pbk)
ISBN: 978-1-59638-850-5 (ePub)
ISBN: 978-1-59638-851-2 (Mobi)

Printed in the United States of America

Library of Congress Cataloging-in-Publication Data

Lelek, Jeremy, 1973-
  Post-traumatic stress disorder : recovering hope / Jeremy Lelek. -- 1st ed.
    pages cm. -- (The Gospel for real life)
  Includes bibliographical references.
  ISBN 978-1-59638-421-7 (pbk.)
  1. Post-traumatic stress disorder--Patients--Religious life. 2. Post-traumatic stress disorder--Religious aspects--Christianity. 3. Fear--Religious aspects--Christianity. I. Title.
  BV4910.45.L45 2013
  248.8'6--dc23
                                                  2013004229

NOTE TO THE READER

Addressing a complex topic such as *Post-Traumatic Stress Disorder* (PTSD) within the confines of a brief booklet is a daunting task, to say the least. The instances of trauma that spark this struggle are vast, and the horrors it exudes in the mind are beyond what many of us can imagine. The symptoms associated with this diagnosis epitomize the notion of intense, paralyzing fear while reminding us (i.e., family, friends, helpers) of our duty to offer an abundance of compassion and love to those suffering from this debilitating problem.

The booklet you are about to read points to the unquestionable fundamentals of life—fundamentals we cannot afford to ignore if we hope to navigate this issue well. It incorporates the redemptive narrative of creation, fall, and redemption as they relate to the experiences associated with PTSD. This diagnosis, as it is conceptualized by our culture, is rooted in an existential threat—the experience of being confronted with danger, a threat to one's physical well-being, or even a close encounter with death. These are things to which the gospel courageously speaks. As such, this booklet attempts to guide readers back to the essence of their existence in an effort to help them recapture the peace and contentment inherent in functioning with God's glory as their greatest aim.

There are numerous resources that offer a myriad of methods to address the specific symptoms associated with PTSD. These methods can assist victims to gain control over things like panic, rage, and uncontrollable flashbacks. Without question, such resources should be utilized to the glory of God. This booklet does not attempt to cover similar methods in great detail.

Instead, it provides a sound worldview to understand yourself, your suffering, and most importantly God as you wade through the numerous struggles associated with this diagnosis. The ideas offered here will serve to undergird everything you do as you seek to address the symptoms associated with PTSD. They will lead you to your place in the world and point you to a God whose commitment to your good will strike you with awe. Soak in these truths as healing water to your soul, and in faith seek to apply each principle. May his Spirit grant you everything you need for this journey!

*

A night that will forever be etched in the depths of my consciousness is September 10, 2001. My wife and I were ten months into raising our first child. Since we were wrestling through the scarcity of funds brought on by my menial practice as a counseling intern, that evening found me at home babysitting my son while my precious wife supplemented our income as a hardworking labor-and-delivery nurse. It was a time of challenge, but for two youngsters trying to make our way in the big city of Fort Worth, it was an exciting season in our lives.

I remember the evening well. I was watching the opening game of *Monday Night Football*, and the Giants were facing off with the Broncos. The cool breeze of fall crept through the raised windows in our tiny living room, and I held our baby boy while he gulped down his final bottle before bedtime. Peace was in the air. Staring into my son's innocent-looking eyes, I had one of those moments when I was keenly aware of God's infinite love in our lives. I remember thinking, *This is going to be an amazing year. Thank you, Father, for all you have given us.* I don't remember if I finished the football game, but I am certain I went to bed that night with a hopeful heart.

The next morning began with my common routine of coffee and prayer. Shortly thereafter, I turned on the television to catch the news before heading off to a full day of counseling. On the screen I saw a place where my wife and I had been the day after our wedding, just three years before. Something was different though. The tall pristine buildings we had visited were engulfed in smoke, and at that moment I witnessed the chaos of 9/11 unfold before my eyes. The hope and calm of the night before was engulfed by horror and sadness. The joy of just a few hours earlier, brought on by thoughts of raising my son, were replaced with literal terror as I thought of him having to grow up in such a wretched world. As with all Americans that day, my life changed.

I saw my first client that morning, my mind barely able to focus. He was struggling with issues related to schizophrenia and was far more concerned about the government microphones that were recording our sessions than anything happening in New York or Washington, DC. As I listened to him elaborate on his latest conspiracy theory, pregnant with paranoia, I journeyed into my own existential nightmare. What was my life going to be like in this new age of terror? Was my family going to experience the agony of a biological or chemical attack? Would we ever step foot on an airplane again to go visit my in-laws in New York? Was the economy going to crash? Was God going to let America be decimated by evil? I admit I was in a complete state of self-protection with my kingdom at the forefront.

WHAT IS POST-TRAUMATIC STRESS DISORDER?

Post-Traumatic Stress Disorder (PTSD) is described by psychiatry as

the development of characteristic symptoms following exposure to an extreme traumatic stressor involving direct personal experience of an event that involves actual or threatened death or serious injury, or other threat to one's physical integrity; or witnessing an event that involves death, injury, or a threat to the physical integrity of another person.[1]

A few examples cited in the *Diagnostic and Statistical Manual of Mental Disorders* include serving in military combat, being a victim of violent personal assault, being kidnapped, being taken hostage, seeing or experiencing a terrorist attack, being tortured, being incarcerated as a prisoner of war or in a concentration camp, or being involved in an automobile accident.[2] As one reads the list of potential contexts in which a person can develop symptoms cited within this diagnosis, it becomes apparent that PTSD is not reserved exclusively to the combat soldier; instead, it has the potential to touch anyone who has experienced a strong sense of threat to his or her physical well-being. As a biblical counselor, it is important to seriously consider the question, Does the Bible bear any weight in helping someone who has such a complex diagnosis as PTSD?

As we begin answering this question, it is important to remember that the label PTSD simply explains a person's behavior and thought processes while taking into account the context in which such patterns developed. In essence it describes a profoundly intense response to a profoundly intense, danger-provoking experience. These responses are centered in fear, terrifying vulnerability, and an exacerbated awareness of not being in control. They are often involuntary and may include things like "recurrent and intrusive distressing recollections of the event, including images, thoughts, or perceptions," "recurrent distressing dreams of the event," "acting or feeling as if the traumatic event were recurring," "efforts to avoid thoughts, feelings, or

1. *Diagnostic and Statistical Manual of Mental Disorders*, 4th ed. (Washington, DC: American Psychological Association, 2000), 463.
2. Ibid.

conversations associated with the trauma," or "difficulty falling or staying asleep."[3] While some of these responses feel completely involuntary, it is important for the individual to embrace the reality that they are responses nonetheless, implying the hope that a different response is possible. As such, by God's power and grace a person can respond increasingly in wholeness, love, and integrity. However, for the person experiencing the impulsive reactions associated with the label PTSD, these responses seem almost impossible. Let's consider one reason for this.

FIGHT OR FLIGHT: OUR AUTO-RESPONSE

As human beings we have been gifted with sensory perceptions designed to assist us in times of danger. When we are faced with a potentially harmful situation, these systems create a response commonly referred to as "fight or flight." This response is highly physiological and correlates with a part of the brain called the hypothalamus. So if a person is threatened, the brain releases large amounts of chemicals such as adrenaline, noradrenaline, and cortisol, causing the heart rate to significantly increase and the respiratory system to kick into overdrive, creating enormous amounts of energy in preparation for the individual to either fight off the threat or run from it. I remember once seeing a video of a helicopter crash in which the pilot was trapped in the wreckage mostly submerged under water. He was literally seconds from death. People were scrambling everywhere when suddenly a large man ran to the helicopter, knelt down, grabbed the bottom of what was left of the huge aircraft, and lifted it just enough for the pilot to break free. He did this all by himself! This seemingly supernatural surge of strength was due, in large part, to the chemical reactions associated with the "fight or flight" response.

3. Ibid., 468.

While this response has been wired into our physiology by our gracious Creator and is a good and wonderful attribute when danger is present, it cannot become *the* dominant factor in shaping our faith, because the faculties that create it are flawed. Our physiology cannot be allowed to overly influence the ultimate values of our lives. If it does become the final determinant to understanding our struggle, then that for which it was designed (e.g., safety, protection, and security) will become the chief end of our existence. We will become consumed with escaping danger or avoiding potential harm, exacerbating the symptoms typically associated with PTSD.

If our physiological reactions to perceived danger hijack our conceptual understanding of the problem, then anytime we feel threatened and experience the intense bodily responses to such perceived threat, our minds will become conditioned by this physiological reality in such a way that we will yield our lives to it with unfettered faith. We will begin to trust our impulses over anything else in the world and find ourselves lashing out in anger or collapsing under the grip of a mind-blowing panic attack. We will, in effect, be committing ourselves to a profoundly confused existential state in which the ultimate hope and glory for our lives is our own self-protection. To counter this trend we will need to remember that our bodies are broken by the influence of sin. Therefore we must acknowledge that even complex systems legitimately designed by God to protect us—systems that wield powerful physical influences on our bodies and minds—do not deserve the ultimate position of authority in our hearts. They can't be trusted indiscriminately.

Principles of Perseverance

1. I recognize that I am desperate for the grace of Jesus Christ and the power of the Holy Spirit in this battle. I acknowledge the wisdom of Jesus, who said, "Watch and

pray that you may not enter into temptation. The spirit indeed is willing, but the flesh is weak" (Matt. 26:41).

2. I will seek God with expectancy to help me remember that my body (i.e., brain) is broken and marred by the influence of sin and the fall (Gen. 3).

3. I must realize that Christ's life is in me through the Holy Spirit and, therefore, as Jesus promises, new life and strength can and will affect my innermost being, right in the deepest places of my pain and trauma. (See John 7:37–39; 1 Cor. 6:19–20; Gal. 2:20. See also Eph. 4:24; Col. 3:10.)

4. I must realize that while my physical responses to a perceived threat feel legitimate, it is likely I am depending more on my own perception and wisdom than on the wisdom offered to me by God.

5. I will seek God with expectancy for the strength and discernment to walk wisely in my brokenness. I will pray that my faith in the Lord (not my body) will begin to control my perceptions and responses in this fallen world.

THE NEED FOR SOUND WISDOM AND DISCRETION

PTSD should not be considered exclusively a psychiatric disorder or a biological issue. Actually, viewing it as such would be quite limiting to the process of healing and ultimate holiness. In essence, the struggles associated with PTSD are existential in nature. What I mean by this is that PTSD has much to do with one's view of existence and being in the world. This brings our conversation into the arena of theology and philosophy and circumvents the idea that it is a mere biological phenomenon. The fear of death or losing control, the rage that bursts forth from the soul due to a perceived or actual threat, is a human response to danger. While it is a seemly uncontrollable biological response, in part it is a response of the soul. While this booklet is not intended to minimize the diagnosis of PTSD, it *is* an attempt to explore the existential realities underlying this struggle. And for us to gain proper perspective on these realities, it will be imperative to consult Scripture as our basis for understanding self and our purpose and place in the cosmos.

In the end, healing from trauma will require a deep faith in something or Someone that transcends our finite existence. This is because on our best days, left to ourselves, our vision of reality is muddled as though we were peering through dark, faded glass (1 Cor. 13:12). This is the case even if trauma is not part of our lives. Our understanding and ability to perceive accurately is limited, and being traumatized magnifies these limitations. Hence our desperate need for eternal wisdom in order to shape a proper perspective! Consider these words from the book of Proverbs:

> The LORD by wisdom founded the earth;
>   by understanding he established the heavens;
> by his knowledge the deeps broke open,
>   and the clouds drop down the dew.
> My son, do not lose sight of these—
>   keep sound wisdom and discretion,
> and they will be life for your soul
>   and adornment for your neck.
> Then you will walk on your way securely,
>   and your foot will not stumble.
> If you lie down, you will not be afraid;
>   when you lie down, your sleep will be sweet.
> Do not be afraid of sudden terror
>   or of the ruin of the wicked, when it comes,
> for the LORD will be your confidence
>   and will keep your foot from being caught. (Prov. 3:19–26)

The author of this proverb is revealing to us the pathway wherein we can walk securely and lie down without fear. He is pointing us to a state of being where our sleep will be sweet and the Lord will be our confidence. And what does he point us to for such peace of mind? It is sound wisdom and discretion.

James shares something similar regarding the topic of wisdom. His words are poignant for the person who suffers under the vacillating impulses of anxiety, fear, and anger on the one hand, and desires to stop these emotions on the other. In the context of trials and suffering (James 1:2–4) he writes,

> If any of you lacks wisdom, let him ask God, who gives generously to all without reproach, and it will be given him. But let him ask in faith, with no doubting, for the one who doubts is like a wave of the sea that is driven and tossed by the wind. For that person must not suppose that he will receive anything from the Lord; he is a double-minded man, unstable in all his ways. (James 1:5–8)

James makes it clear that when we face trials and lack wisdom we are not to rest in our own abilities or look inward to ourselves; rather, we are to open our hearts to Someone beyond ourselves. He calls us to open our hearts to God. When we do so, James tells us that God is generous to the one in need! The problem is not that he refuses to grant wisdom to his people. Instead, James points out that problems arise when his wisdom is offered and the one seeking help chooses to doubt rather than believe. James tells us that a refusal to embrace God's wisdom comes at a great price in that such doubting will create profound instability and extreme psychological confusion or, as he calls it, double-mindedness.

You may ask, "So all I have to do is seek God for wisdom and he's going to supernaturally insert that wisdom into my heart? Then my problems with fear, anger, and anxiety will be solved?" That would be easy, wouldn't it? However, it doesn't work that way because wisdom comes from (or through) God's Word, never in isolation from it. While God does guide our lives and hearts, the only assurance we have that we are receiving wisdom genuinely from God is that it is always conditioned and shaped by the Bible, the only foundation for all of life and our thinking. You see, God has already spoken divine wisdom into the world, and that wisdom has been revealed in the form of Scripture. So when we seek wisdom from God, the first place we should begin our search is the Bible.

It is certainly easy in our culture of self-help—with its plethora of books offering the latest tips on happiness and fulfillment—to minimize the wisdom of Scripture. To do so, however, is a destructive mistake. The words of the Bible are not intended for self-help but are given to reveal the selfless one, Jesus Christ. The Bible is not into self-help; it is into Jesus-help. It reveals Jesus. We are told, "And the Word became flesh and dwelt among us, and we have seen his glory, glory as of the only Son from the Father, full of grace and truth" (John 1:14). It reveals to us the One who reorients our hearts on a deeply existential level—the One who brings clarity to life and solidifies our purpose in the world. The Bible contains the very thoughts of the God who made us. It helps us see and live with God in view. It is itself the substance of life. *It must not and cannot be overlooked.* Consider just a few examples of how God esteems his Word.

First, the fatherly instruction of God to the people of Israel.

> And you shall remember the whole way that the LORD your God has led you these forty years in the wilderness, that he might humble you, testing you to know what was in your heart, whether you would keep his commandments or not. And he humbled you and let you hunger and fed you with manna, which you did not know, nor did your fathers know, that he

might make you know that man does not live by bread alone,
but man lives by every word that comes from the mouth of
the Lord. (Deut. 8:2–3)

Or his command to Joshua:

This Book of the Law shall not depart from your mouth, but
you shall meditate on it day and night, so that you may be
careful to do according to all that is written in it. For then
you will make your way prosperous, and then you will have
good success. (Josh. 1:8)

And the enlightening description penned by the author of
Hebrews:

For the word of God is living and active, sharper than any
two-edged sword, piercing to the division of soul and of spirit,
of joints and of marrow, and discerning the thoughts and
intentions of the heart. (Heb. 4:12)

These verses describe the essential nature of the Bible for all
of life. Our souls' survival depends on the Word of God! Our
success in knowing and worshiping God depends on the sacred
Scriptures. And our attempts to accurately understand ourselves
in this world are realized only through this divine book. If, as
the Bible claims, the Word of God is so significant, then our
first step in pursuing wisdom should be to consult it as it applies
to the struggles associated with PTSD.

THE WISDOM OF GOD IN CREATION

You may wonder why I'm mentioning creation in a book on
PTSD. That's a fair question. Since PTSD is linked to the issue
of well-being or the threat to our existence due to trauma, it is
important that we first get our bearings in regard to a biblical

view of ontology (i.e., existence). To do so, we must begin in the beginning.

The Bible tells us that God's attributes, especially his eternal power and divine nature, may be understood "in the things that have been made" (Rom. 1:20). Creation points to God. The majesty of a mountain range or the dazzle of the sun setting beneath the ocean's horizon all point to the power and authorship of God. If you are reading this booklet and have the capacity of awareness that you exist and are reading this booklet, then this too points to God. Your very being screams, "God exists, and as such I am not the final reference point of reality!" Creation puts us in our place. We are not the center of the universe, though we have something in us (sin) that daily seeks to convince us otherwise. Creation points us to the Creator. It vividly reminds us that all existing things are centered in him (or should be)! As the psalmist eloquently exclaims:

> Mountains and all hills,
>   fruit trees and all cedars!
> Beasts and all livestock,
>   creeping things and flying birds!
> Kings of the earth and all peoples,
>   princes and all rulers of the earth!
> Young men and maidens together,
>   old men and children!
> Let them praise the name of the LORD,
>   for his name alone is exalted;
>   his majesty is above earth and heaven. (Ps. 148:9–13)

All that you see every day exists for God's pleasure and glory! *You* were created for his pleasure and glory! Have you ever thought about that? Your life, your blessings, your heartaches, and, yes, even your trauma cannot be minimized as existing in some type of void or impersonal universe. God has spoken to mankind through his Word, and when we understand our lives and existence in light of his Word, it is then that we begin to comprehend what actually is.

This view goes against the notion that "perception is reality" and exposes it as a severely misguided idea. Human perception is distorted reality, and without Scripture as our lens it is a profoundly fractured reality. Trauma will provide a powerful context for you to see life in a fractured way. It will set in motion all sorts of things within your heart that will compete with the glory of your Creator. Trauma will seek to disrupt your understanding of who you are in this world: a creature designed to bellow the glory of the living God with your entire being! Trauma is part of the fracture (suffering), but it is also a catalyst in deepening the fracture because the fears, thoughts, and beliefs that are part of our reaction to trauma have a strong tendency to distract us from the reality of God.

Recognizing the fact that we are creatures fashioned by the hand of God is a beginning point for mending the fracture in our minds (Gen. 1:27). While trauma creates confusion about our existence, understanding our place in the universe (i.e., God's creation) reorients us to the fundamentals of our existence. Life did not originate with us, nor can it be properly understood with our finite understanding. Life is a gift from God. Our limited perceptions do not always capture actuality, because all reality hinges on the power and sovereignty of Another! Any one of us at any given time can badly misconstrue reality. We are entirely dependent on the full and perfect gaze of God. As he views reality, what does he see? If we do not seek a greater perspective than our own, then we have no hope to view our lives and circumstances accurately.

Our ideas do not dictate reality in the sense of determining it. Instead, there exists an objective reality in the cosmos, determined by the immutable nature of God. And while we will never have exhaustive comprehension of it, since we see life as though peering through a dark glass (1 Cor. 13:12), God's Word is sure to serve as a lamp to our feet and a light to our path (Ps. 119:105), offering the guidance and understanding we need to navigate this journey wisely and well!

The central and constant light that all of Scripture will shed on your path is that God and his glory will always need to serve as our greatest aim. We saw in the verse above that, as creatures, we must submit to the idea that "his name alone is exalted." Trauma rushes in upon this reality and makes it, at best, a secondary purpose in our lives. If we get this piece out of order, then the entire foundation of our understanding (both of ourselves and the world) crumbles into dust, leaving us to wade through the sinking sand shifting beneath our feet. And while most believers can say, "I know I'm a creature and am called to worship God," the challenge before us is to determine whether we live this out as though it were true. We may know the right answer, but are our hearts captured and thrilled by this reality? Has the brokenness we've experienced influenced us to minimize or doubt or even forget this truth? After trauma, if we hope to get our minds back on track, one of the most important goals to set for ourselves is to recall and embrace our ultimate purpose in this world while seeking God's wisdom to navigate the process of healing. We must contemplate our place in the world, as creatures designed to glory in Another, and begin to approach our life and struggles from this vantage point.

Principles of Perseverance

1. Read Psalm 148. Write down the verses/phrases that place God at the center of all praise. Recognize the purpose of all creation: praise to God! Is such praise your ultimate goal at this time? Why or why not?

2. What tragedy or trauma in your life trumps the necessity for you to praise God? Why might you justify a refusal to praise him?

3. Search your heart and seek to understand what is blinding you from your purpose. What longings capture you? Safety? Control? Security?

4. Formulate a purpose for today that is centered in God's glory. Write it down. How will you seek to worship God in your life today? As you seek to overcome the symptoms associated with PTSD, let God's glory be your chief aim!

5. As you read the Scriptures regularly, do so with this question in mind: how does this passage shape the purpose of my life?

6. While you may not completely understand why you have had to endure so much suffering, you can be assured that God's purposes for you have not been thwarted. Pray along these lines: "Lord, help me recognize that my sufferings will ultimately serve as an instrument designed to bring glory to your name and to form me into a person of greater faith, obedience, and love. Give me a heart to rejoice!"

THE WISDOM OF GOD IN SIN AND SUFFERING

At this point it may be tempting to think that this booklet offers some sort of extreme view in that we began with creation and its sole purpose to glorify God. However, if we fail to understand our origin and therefore our position in the world (i.e., creatures of God designed to worship him), we will lose our bearing and drift into extremely dangerous territory. It is a territory where self becomes the center point of our being.

Actually, the creation story reveals to us how we even got to this place as human beings where self is the center point. For this story not only reveals the splendor of creation and the Creator behind it, but it also exposes the horror of the fall. God created the first man, Adam (Gen. 2:7), and then instructed him, "You may surely eat of every tree of the garden, but of the tree of the knowledge of good and evil you shall not eat, for in the day that you eat of it you shall surely die" (Gen. 2:16–17). It was simple. Adam and Eve were free to enjoy everything in God's creation except the tree of the knowledge of good and evil. Had they heeded his command and trusted in his goodwill toward them, they would have fulfilled their purpose as creatures designed to honor and glorify God. However, they failed miserably by doubting and refusing his goodness and wisdom. Why? They refused their purpose in the world to glorify God by trusting in him and submitting to him. They chose to reason without reference to God and his perfect wisdom. The Bible recounts the scene like this:

> Now the serpent was more crafty than any other beast of the field that the LORD God had made. He said to the woman, "Did God actually say, 'You shall not eat of any tree in the garden'?" And the woman said to the serpent, "We may eat of the fruit of the trees in the garden, but God said, 'You shall not eat of the fruit of the tree that is in the midst of the garden, neither shall you touch it, lest you die.'" But the serpent said to the woman, "You will not surely die. For God knows that when you eat of it your eyes will be opened, and you will be like God, knowing good and evil." So when the woman saw that the tree was good for food, and that it was a delight to the eyes, and that the tree was to be desired to make one wise, she took of its fruit and ate, and she also gave some to her husband who was with her, and he ate. Then the eyes of both were opened, and they knew that they were naked. And they sewed fig leaves together and made themselves loincloths. (Gen. 3:1–7)

As a result of this cosmic rebellion, pain and suffering began to plague the earth and mankind became dead in his trespasses (Eph. 2). It was at this point that a human being, for the first time ever, could be exposed to the experience of trauma! Up until that time Adam and Eve were free to fully enjoy the serenity and beauty of all creation without any fear of harm. But their disobedience changed everything. Now the potential for murder, war, rape, and abuse could flourish. Evil had risen, fracturing the entire cosmos! Man's choosing to reject God's wisdom and instead to recreate his own existential reality, centered in self, ushered in the possibility of trauma and pain and literally changed the world as they knew it! Refusing his wisdom always has profound consequences.

This fracture did not simply change things structurally *for* man, making man have to work by the sweat of his brow and making woman have to endure pain in childbirth. It also changed things systemically *in* man. The apostle Paul offers a graphic description of this change.

> They were filled with all manner of unrighteousness, evil, covetousness, malice. They are full of envy, murder, strife, deceit, maliciousness. They are gossips, slanderers, haters of God, insolent, haughty, boastful, inventors of evil, disobedient to parents, foolish, faithless, heartless, ruthless. Though they know God's decree that those who practice such things deserve to die, they not only do them but give approval to those who practice them. (Rom. 1:29–32)

Man was different. Mankind's awareness that he was designed to worship the Creator was hijacked by all sorts of self-centered gratifications. These gratifications served as the fuel for such things as murder, heartlessness, and evil. If we're going to have a genuinely biblical understanding of what is called Post-

Traumatic Stress Disorder, then understanding the implications of this change is essential.

The Invasion of Suffering

Once this great rebellion occurred, the propensity for suffering materialized. Human nature was now ravaged by the corruption of sin, opening the possibility for people to do unthinkable acts of horror against one another. If you want the ultimate answer to why you have experienced suffering or trauma, you will find the root of your answer in the fall, and the origin of the fall was man's rebellion against God and his wisdom. Suffering is a terrible thing. It hurts. It's scary. It often feels unbearable. Yet it is a reality in our lives because humanity fell away from God. Why do men rape women? Why do terrorists fly planes into buildings or ignite bombs to kill civilians? Why do people get drunk, drive their automobiles, and end up killing others? Why do people get cancer and die? Why do maniacs enter movie theaters or malls or schools and go on shooting rampages? The answer to these questions is that our world exists in a fallen, sinful state. Suffering is an existential reality for all mankind, and the Bible offers us the most robust explanation behind this reality. It also tells us much about the God who exists in the midst of suffering.

Suffering and the Watchful Eye of a Good and Just God

I am not sure what circumstances in your life have influenced you to read a book on PTSD. However, I am certain of this: if you have experienced trauma at the hands of another person, God has something to say about it. A comforting reality is that suffering at the hands of another does not go unnoticed. God sees, and he has given us a glimpse of his perspective. Consider the following passages and what they say regarding God's heart towards evil:

> Therefore the wicked will not stand in the judgment,
>   nor sinners in the congregation of the righteous;

for the LORD knows the way of the righteous,
  but the way of the wicked will perish. (Ps. 1:5–6)

The LORD tests the righteous,
  but his soul hates the wicked and the one who loves violence.
Let him rain coals on the wicked;
  fire and sulfur and a scorching wind shall be the portion of
    their cup. (Ps. 11:5–6)

For God will bring every deed into judgment, with every secret
thing, whether good or evil. (Eccl. 12:14)

For the wrath of God is revealed from heaven against all ungod-
liness and unrighteousness of men, who by their unrighteousness suppress the truth. (Rom. 1:18)

Beloved, never avenge yourselves, but leave it to the wrath of
God, for it is written, "Vengeance is mine, I will repay, says
the Lord." (Rom. 12:19)

Let no one deceive you with empty words, for because of these
things the wrath of God comes upon the sons of disobedience.
(Eph. 5:6)

God despises evil with all of his heart. His rage against such
evil is a place of solace for your hurting soul. In considering the
brokenness of the universe and those who have committed evil
against you, seek to remember that their lives and deeds reside in
the hands of a just God. He is committed to confronting all sin
with perfect judgment. While it may be difficult to remember
this fact, pursuing rest in this truth is vital.

Suffering and the Caring Heart of God

Did you know that God is profoundly concerned about your
suffering? If you are a believer in Jesus, here is a stunning truth:

God cares for you! The Bible reveals that King David struggled with this reality to the point of asking,

> When I look at your heavens, the work of your fingers,
>   the moon and the stars, which you have set in place,
> what is man that you are mindful of him,
>   and the son of man that you care for him? (Ps. 8:3–4)

When we consider all that is going on in the universe and in the world, when we look at the millions of people on this earth and all that is going on in their lives, it is tempting to forget the piercing gaze of God. It is tempting to feel isolated from him. Yet, in actuality, he is intimately present and genuinely concerned about his people. Peter points to this when he encourages believers to

> Humble yourselves, therefore, under the mighty hand of God so that at the proper time he may exalt you, casting all your anxieties on him, *because he cares for you*. (1 Peter 5:6–7, emphasis added)

You, too, must remember this. No matter how deeply you have been traumatized, God possesses an incomprehensible care for you in your pain!

God Is Committed to Transforming You in Suffering

Have you ever heard the "Christian" adage, "God loves you and has a wonderful plan for your life"? Just typing those words makes me cringe, because what is often meant is a man-centered distortion of God's actual plan for believers.

Often when we hear these words we think of God creating a special plan that is going to give us a special place in the world so we can feel special. The reality, however, is that God *does* have a special plan for the believer, but it's not about making us feel special. It is not a plan designed to make much of us, but it is designed to help us make much of him. The "special" referred to in this statement is not a position of prominence for ourselves; rather, it is better understood as working in a specific way for a distinct purpose.

In a general sense God's plan for all his children is the same plan. It is the transformation of your entire being. Here is something that is a significant fact for you as you seek to overcome trauma in your life: God is committed to transforming you through the process (Rom. 8:28–29). In all circumstances, his aim is to transform you into a child of glory. Such a process will ultimately cause you to reflect genuine, perfect humanity. Why is that important? Consider the following: Do you want to exhibit unshakable faith in the Father as Jesus did? Do you have a desire to face trial and hardship with the hope and power Jesus exhibited? Do you want to view the storms in your life with the same calm and confidence as he? Do you want to possess the ability to think like Jesus? If so, you will have to endure the process of being reshaped and molded into his image. This is God's plan for you, and he is committed to accomplishing it in both your joy and your pain (1 Thess. 4:3–7; Titus 2:11–14; James 1:2–4).

The Impact of Sin

As I mentioned earlier, the fall changed humanity systemically. What I mean by this is that humans are now born sinners and their innate propensity is only toward sin. This sin is a cunning enemy. It is often subtle and deceitful, and its inertia directs the heart away from God. It is sin that clouds the mind to the pure goodness and perfection of God (even for believers). It is the variable within tribulation that influences the confusion of mind to ask such a thing as, "Why did God let this happen to me?" or make the statement, "A good God would never allow such hurtful things!" The fact that I make these claims may surprise you, and I am in no way implying that it is unnatural to cry out to God when trauma strikes your life. As I've already outlined, God is deeply concerned about your experience. The

Bible is filled with people whose raw emotions are almost tangible, and this *should* be an aspect of our relating to God. Yet, when genuine doubt and contempt for God enter your heart, it is sin that escorts them in. When painful circumstances influence us to forget our design and position (as revealed in the creation story), and contribute to our tendency to glory in anything other than God, then the influence of sin and its brokenness are at work. If you want to accurately conceptualize any response to life, especially responses that do not bring glory to God, then sin must be included. Let's consider how sin is continually impacting our lives.

Sin causes our thinking to become futile and our hearts to become darkened (Rom. 1:21). Sin impacts our thought life. It influences our minds to lose proper perspective. It darkens our understanding to genuine reality (Eph. 4:18). It causes us to misunderstand and misconstrue our circumstances. Our thinking and belief systems can be profoundly tainted by the influence of this unrelenting enemy!

Sin influences us to trust our own wisdom above God's wisdom (Rom. 1:22). The Bible tells us that it is the fool who says in his heart God does not exist (Ps. 14:1). While many reading this book have placed a genuine faith in Jesus, sin can influence even the most faithful in Christ to live, think, perceive, and evaluate existence as though God is not real. Think about it: when you snap at your child or grumble because you have to work, you are literally living as though God doesn't exist. If you were operating under those circumstances with his presence in mind, you would likely choose your words more wisely when correcting your child and offer a genuine prayer of gratitude that God has granted his provisions to you through your job. Sin can literally influence us to believe that our wisdom supersedes God's.

Sin causes our hearts to replace the glory of God with the glory of idols (Rom. 1:23). One significant reason we began our discussion with creation is because it serves to remind us that we are created for the purposes of Another. We are created for God's glory. Sin, however, distracts us from this and causes our hearts to lust after things other than God. Our glory takes center stage as we yield our hearts to passions that divert our motives from bringing glory to Christ alone. In the case of trauma, these passions can take on the form of "innocence," as the person traumatized can easily begin to rationalize and justify a sinful coveting for safety, security, and peace. This is indeed a difficult dilemma, but one that cannot be ignored.

Sin creates inner confusion (Rom. 7:14–24). So often the process of change can feel like one step forward and two steps back. A person can be 100 percent mentally determined to change certain patterns, only to fail over and over again. Sin plays a role in this experience. Paul expressed it this way:

> So I find it to be a law that when I want to do right, evil lies close at hand. For I delight in the law of God, in my inner being, but I see in my members another law waging war against the law of my mind and making me captive to the law of sin that dwells in my members. (Rom. 7:21–23)

For the unbeliever, this dynamic is absolute slavery. For the Christian, this dynamic is part of persevering in the faith—a faith that is rooted in none other than Jesus Christ (Rom. 7:25). The person diagnosed with PTSD can feel profoundly determined to stop certain behaviors associated with this label, but sin is relentless in its influence to pull us away from truth, and more significantly, the God of truth.

Sin is agenda driven and hostile to God (Rom. 8:7). If you are committed to understanding yourself biblically, then you have to come to grips with the fact that, as a fallen creature, you are not a neutral being. You are not autonomous, and becoming so is not even possible. Your heart has allegiances, and those allegiances are shaped by your values and desires. These values are deeply spiritual. As individuals still influenced by sin, we have the remains in our lives of our former hostility toward God. Actually, if you are a Christian, there is a war between your new life in the Spirit and your old life in the flesh (Gal. 5:16–18). We must (and he enables us to) put off all that remains in us of our former life and put on the new life that is ours in Christ Jesus (Col. 3:5–13). Though we were darkness, we are now light in the Lord (Eph. 5:8). We are now the temple of God, bought with the price of Christ's blood, and we do not belong to ourselves anymore (1 Cor. 6:19). Because you belong to Christ, the Holy Spirit lives in you, and he is committed to transforming you completely (2 Cor. 3:18).

Sin is the major problem and it comes from within (Gal. 5:19–21). When the religious leaders claimed that Jesus' disciples were defiled because they ate with unwashed hands, Jesus taught that evil does not come to us from outside; it comes from within.

> Do you not see that whatever goes into the mouth passes into the stomach and is expelled? But what comes out of the mouth proceeds from the heart, and this defiles a person. For out of the heart come evil thoughts, murder, adultery, sexual immorality, theft, false witness, slander. These are what defile a person. But to eat with unwashed hands does not defile anyone. (Matt. 15:17–20)

So often, in our culture of psychology, we are prone to ascribing behaviors such as fits of rage and anxiety to elaborate disorders or chemical reactions. However, if we are seeking to understand our hearts and our responses at a fundamental level, acknowledgement of the reality of the construct of sin and its influence on our thinking, desiring, and behaving is essential.

Sin is deceitful (Eph. 4:22). Sin disorients our minds. Sin so often influences through its deceitful nature. Sin turns the world upside down. It can influence us to genuinely value being loved (man-centered wisdom) over loving others (God-ordained wisdom), to cherish being respected over offering humble service, or to trust self rather than God. Sin takes good things and magnifies them to incoherent, inappropriate positions within our hearts.

The person who has come face to face with trauma cannot ignore the cunning influence sin wields on our perspectives. Paul instructs Christians to "put off your old self, which belongs to your former manner of life and is corrupt through deceitful desires" (Eph. 4:22). Deceit is an attribute of sin, and it can have devastating effects on the mind. The more a person places faith in such deceit, the more corruption flourishes, pushing the individual ever further into the clutches of deceit. For example, if my heart deceives me to believe that the ultimate hope in my life is relational safety, then I will manage my life in such a way that protecting myself from being hurt by others becomes that in which I glory most. I may begin with allowing only those who give me a sense of safety to be part of my life. It doesn't take long, however, for me to realize that even these individuals have the capacity to hurt and offend me. As such, I create all sorts of boundaries by which my friends must abide in order to be a part of my life. Before long I become an isolated, critical, hypersensitive hermit without any genuine friendships. I'm a control freak who will allow into my life only people who are willing to bow to my demands of safety. Due to the deceitful nature of sin, my relationships are no longer centered in the glory of God and the love of my neighbor, but in the perpetual lies of my darkened heart.

These are just a few examples of sin's influence on us as we confront suffering. The fall has a profound role in conceptualizing our struggles, even those with elaborate names such as *Post-Traumatic Stress Disorder*. It is important to remember that the profession from which PTSD derives its name, the profession that provides the orthodoxy for understanding the criteria of PTSD, is one in which the ideas of creation and fall are not considered. The research you read in various books may be extremely helpful in identifying certain themes, brain functions, and methods to improve symptoms, but none of them originate from a theocentric frame of reference. The result of this major oversight is that the most fundamental aspects of who you are as a human being are missed, and your greatest Advocate, Jesus Christ, becomes a side note in your journey.

Principles of Perseverance

1. *Identify your futile thoughts.* How has trauma influenced your thinking? What beliefs have you adopted "post trauma" that were not present prior to the event? What beliefs influence fear, anger, or the need to control? How do any of these beliefs expose your beliefs about God? Read Psalm 139:1–16. Extract truths from this psalm and use them to begin to reorient your belief system about yourself, life, and the ever-present reality of God. Jot down these new beliefs and ask the Holy Spirit to implant them into the depths of your soul.

2. *Recognize where your wisdom is overriding God's wisdom.* Read Jeremiah 17:5–9. What type of life does the prophet promise if you trust in man (either others or yourself)?

What does trusting man produce? What does trusting God produce? Write out three ways you will seek to trust God with your life in the coming week.

3. *Resist covetous and evil desires.* Desiring safety is very appropriate, but worshiping safety is not. Read Ephesians 4:22–24. What desires are you following that may be deceiving you? How is walking according to such desires producing corruption in your mind? In your relationships? What desires will you seek to "put on" during the coming week?

4. *Rest in Jesus.* Overcoming any extreme issue is no simple task. Don't allow "victory over your symptoms" to become the place where you find hope and rest. Consistency in productive behavior or right thinking cannot be your source of comfort. That position is reserved for Another. Read Psalm 62:1–5 and Romans 8:1–2. Consider what it means to find hope in God alone. List five practical ways you will seek to rest in God when you are struggling with symptoms associated with PTSD.

Redeeming Wisdom

The wonderful news of the gospel is that the story does not end with the fall. Instead, the fall paves the way for the climax of this divine story by ushering in the narrative of redemption and our great and blessed Redeemer, Jesus Christ! And wisdom regarding the person and nature of Jesus is imperative if we are to have any hope whatsoever in the midst of sin and suffering in this world. If we are to make any sense of our existence (suffering and all), we must view it through the lens of the gospel.

You see, trauma has the potential to develop a profoundly myopic outlook for its victim. It is an outlook by which a person's entire life becomes defined by the traumatic event. People begin to say things like, "I can't ride in a car when someone else drives, because I was in a horrible car accident." "My view of men is that they're all snakes. Since being raped, this is simply the way I feel." "Since being deployed and having to engage in combat, if I feel threatened in any way, I can't help but respond with rage." These are revealing statements in that much of what each person believes and does is attributed to the trauma they have experienced. Their life is now actually trauma-centric, in that everything they do and think is centered in the traumatic event. Each one is blinded to absolute reality, since they diminish the defining point of their life to a traumatic event.

In truth, life is not centered in a traumatic moment. Remember Psalm 148, where the author beckons all creation to exalt God alone? Or Psalm 95:6, in which the psalmist invites us, "Oh come, let us worship and bow down; let us kneel before the Lord, our Maker!" The psalmist's invitation is not a call to a mere moment of bowing and worshiping; rather, it is to be the continual position of our hearts—hearts that are kneeling before God, worshiping him moment by moment throughout each and every day. These are fundamental, existential realities! The grandeur of the gospel narrative, of God's rescuing his people in mercy and love, and of the unspeakable honor to relate to the Lord cannot be hijacked by a mere sentence of horror in our life story!

We must remember that our trauma is a sentence in the story—it is not *the* story. We can make anything in our lives the focal point of our stories. Pursuing wealth, the perfect marriage, perfect children, or fitness—all of these have the capacity to hijack the real story. Trauma has that capacity too! However, none of these things are the overriding themes of the narrative. Instead, the sentences that make up our individual lives only make sense in the context of the true narrative, the story of redemption as portrayed in the Bible.

Let me give you an example of the gospel narrative being hijacked by a sentence in the story. I once watched a documentary of a man who was struggling horribly with alcohol abuse. He had tragically lost his young son in an auto accident two years prior. He was the driver of the car when the accident happened. My heart broke as I saw him lie in his darkened bedroom day after day, only to come out in the evenings when he would start bingeing on beer and wine. He had a wife and another baby boy, but that didn't matter to him. He was consumed by something else. The scene in the documentary that gripped me most unfolded as one evening he was lying on the couch in his living room, crying, drinking, wailing, drinking, sobbing, and then drinking more. His dear wife sat on the couch absolutely paralyzed by his behavior. His living two-year-old son was crawling around on the floor, whimpering, simply wanting his father to hold him. Dad ignored his precious baby's gestures for affection. Instead of wrapping his arms around his crying boy, he stumbled over to a shelf where he grabbed a tiny urn containing his deceased son's ashes. He lifted up the urn, glared into the camera through his swollen, tearful eyes, and screamed, "My life is over! See this [holding up the urn], this was my life!" He fell to his knees, urn in one hand, a bottle of beer in the other, and melted into the floor in absolute anguish.[4]

No one would deny that this man had experienced trauma. But two years into his battle he was still ravaged by an extreme form of existential confusion. He had lost perspective on life. Why? It was clear to me as I watched. He was allowing a tragic sentence in his life story (i.e., the death of his son) to become the dominating theme of his story. He was constricting his entire life and God-ordained purpose into a sentence, a moment, a season in his life, and he was missing the real story completely! Each night he drank himself into oblivion and worshiped at the shrine of the dead. While the

---

4. Paraphrased from an episode of A&E's *Intervention*.

entire creation was constantly echoing the glory of God, this man sat, night after night, in a darkened room confining his existence to a five-ounce urn of ash. He adopted the sentence of his son's death as the story that would shape his life. Just as the apostle Paul warned, as this man set his mind on the things of the flesh (his version of his own story), it brought death to his very soul (Rom. 8:6).

Had he sought to operate in the real story, he would have pursued his identity as worshiper of God (Ps. 95:6). Though grief, sadness, and agony would have been close companions in his journey, they would not have become his slave masters. He would have remembered the bigger story as highlighted by the apostle Paul, who said, "For since we believe that Jesus died and rose again, even so, through Jesus, God will bring with him those who have fallen asleep" (1 Thess. 4:14). He would have wrestled through his sadness and fulfilled his creation purpose to worship by loving God and neighbor (Luke 10:27). As such, he would have been eager to sow comfort and love into the life of his wife and living son!

He would allow his son's death (a painful reality) to point him to the context in which that sentence in his life took place. The context of a fallen world (Gen. 3), the context that he had the privilege of being part of God's story (Ps. 139:16), the context that he was created for the glory of Another (Ps. 147:10–11), the context of the vanity of life without God (Eccl. 1:14), the context of God's goodness and love (Ps. 136:1), the context of God his Savior (John 3:16), the context of God who works in all things (even tragedy) to transform his own into children of glory (Rom. 8:28–29), the context of a Savior committed to the full redemption and healing of his children (Phil. 1:6; James 1:2–3). These realities would have shaped his existence (assuming he was a believer) and would have served as amazing companions to help him heal from such an unthinkable disaster.

If these narrative themes were dominant in his heart, then the sentence of tragedy that struck his life would not have smothered out the greater narrative at play, and his life would likely not have been so hopeless and miserable. This man attempted to usurp a power he did not possess in that he chose to write the conclusion of his own life. In so doing, he got the story all wrong and missed a profound opportunity to glory in the true Author of his life!

Principles of Perseverance

1. Has the trauma you experienced become the defining point of your life? Does the trauma influence you to alter or structure your life in any way? If so, how?

2. Consider the idea that your trauma is part of your life story but not the crux of your life story. It is a sentence, not the totality of the narrative. Now read 2 Corinthians 1:8–10 and consider the following:

   a. What were the difficulties Paul mentions in these verses? These make up the "sentences" of his own life.

   b. What emotions did he initially experience? Notice, Paul was not superhuman. He experienced difficult emotions.

   c. In verse 9, what is the explanation Paul gives for having to experience these things? This explanation points to the larger redemptive story—it is what made sense of his life experiences.

   d. In verse 10, how does deliverance from peril impact Paul's faith?

3. Take out a sheet of paper, and write out your life story as it pertains to your trauma. Include the experience, the feelings, and the mental struggles (just as Paul did). However, don't stop there. Imitate Paul (in v. 9) and include

the larger redemptive narrative in your story. What are the eternal truths from the Bible that are relevant to your story? Include themes such as your role as worshiper, God as your protector, his mercy and grace, the work of the Holy Spirit, your transformation for his glory, etc. If you need a jumpstart in your thinking, consider the following passages: Psalm 23; 37; 121; 139; Romans 8:26–39; 1 Thessalonians 5:23–24; 1 Peter 2:11; 3:8–4:2.

4. Share your story with others as the Lord provides you the strength to do so. Your story (centered in God's narrative of redemption) has the potential to minister hope into the lives of many others who are suffering.

THE FOUNDER OF OUR SALVATION

Now let's return our thoughts to the main character in this grand redemptive narrative, Jesus Christ. The author of Hebrews penned the following:

It has been testified somewhere,

"What is man, that you are mindful of him,
    or the son of man, that you care for him?
You made him for a little while lower than the angels;
    you have crowned him with glory and honor,
    putting everything in subjection under his feet."

Now in putting everything in subjection to him, he left nothing outside his control. At present, we do not yet see everything in subjection to him. But we see him who for a little while was made lower than the angels, namely Jesus, crowned with glory and honor because of the suffering of death, so that by the grace of God he might taste death for everyone.

For it was fitting that he, for whom and by whom all things exist, in bringing many sons to glory, should make the founder of their salvation perfect through suffering. (Heb. 2:6–10)

Here the writer of Hebrews enters into the celebration of Psalm 8, a celebration of God's gracious gift in making man ruler over all things in this world. However, in Hebrews 2:8 he also taps into the existential reality of being human in that our experience in this world does not look as though everything is in subjection to us. We look and feel like slaves in many ways, not kings; life is so out of control. The experiences of trauma such as violent abuse or coming face to face with death convince us that life is utterly beyond our control. But in this brokenness the author emphasizes an astounding reality. In a world where "we do not yet see everything in subjection to him," he emphasizes the only place wherein we may find hope. He focuses our attention on a deep reality. It is the reality that we do not have to fear death (or any type of trauma), because the One who is crowned with glory and honor because of the suffering of death has tasted death for everyone! This is a death that exceeds in horror anything you could imagine.

Christ, the Creator of all that exists, because he was willing to allow his own creation to unleash extreme cruelty on him, has rescued you from the most traumatic experience known to man (the wrath and rejection of God). He accomplished this by tasting death on your behalf so that you will never have to drink from such a bitter cup (Matt. 26:42)! Instead, through his reigning, finished work, he will eventually bring us to true, final, complete, and glorious kingship. We have hope of deliverance from all trauma, and hopeful restoration in kingly glory!

To help you understand what I'm referring to, consider this for a moment. Imagine experiencing the violation and cruelty of trauma, but in a world where such an experience is perpetual without end! Imagine an existence completely void of the feelings of hope and comfort or a simple moment of relief. Imagine a life where you're not even granted the temporal escape afforded by sleep, but where you are tormented day and night, night and day without end. Even more terrifying, it is an existence where Jesus is not there to comfort you! I can't think of anything more dreadful. It is *this* terrifying trauma that trumps all other forms of trauma, and it is *the* ultimate trauma from which you have been mercifully rescued, assuming you are a believer in Jesus. And this is only possible because Jesus chose to take upon himself the rejection and wrath we deserve, tasting death on our behalf, so that we might be made children of glory. As such, we do not face a future of torment, but one where we will forever dine with the Prince of Peace! It is a hopeful thing to consider that Jesus has already rescued us from the most horrifying trauma possible, eternal separation from him.

Your trauma (a sentence in the greater story), which is to be taken seriously, cannot be allowed to erase the broader story of your existence. It is the story in which we absolutely deserve the wrath and justice of God, but have been mercifully rescued from it. The trauma is not the story from which creation and reality gleans its meaning; it is a sentence within that greater story (the story of redemption). It cannot serve as the core of your identity. It is not your ultimate context. You cannot allow your pain to be the final lens through which you interpret your experiences as a human being. If you do, you will live a life consumed by distortions.

God is your ultimate context, and just as it was in the garden of Eden, only by viewing your life from his eternal vantage point will you be able to see accurately (though not perfectly). Your trauma does not deserve the weight of being your chief reference point. Instead, it vividly points you to a greater story in which the founder of your faith rescues you from your trauma! Seek to broaden your vision to see the entirety of your existence (in the context of the grand story of redemption), and work to resist the temptation to allow evil (e.g., trauma) to be the defining point that dominates the story of your life. Life is not about your trauma; it is about the

One who has liberated you from the most horrifying trauma imaginable! You have been rescued. Seek to live life to celebrate your freedom, and, most importantly, glory in the One who purchased that freedom for you!

OUR MERCIFUL AND SYMPATHETIC HIGH PRIEST

Another relevant aspect of Jesus' character resides in his immensely personal nature. Unlike the mystic gods or "energies" of Eastern philosophy and religion, Jesus is a person, and he relates to us as such. The author of Hebrews beautifully displays the glory of this reality, writing,

> Since therefore the children share in flesh and blood, he himself likewise partook of the same things, that through death he might destroy the one who has the power of death, that is, the devil, and deliver all those who through fear of death were subject to lifelong slavery. For surely it is not angels that he helps, but he helps the offspring of Abraham. Therefore he had to be made like his brothers in every respect, so that he might become a merciful and faithful high priest in the service of God, to make propitiation for the sins of the people. For because he himself has suffered when tempted, he is able to help those who are being tempted. (Heb. 2:14–18)

Jesus knows the experience of trauma! He knows what it's like to exist as flesh and blood. He willingly invaded his fractured creation in order to partake of the pain of suffering, engaging the battle with temptation so that he "might become a merciful and faithful high priest in the service of God"! Can you believe that? Jesus gets you! He gets your pain! He gets your agony! He subjected himself to the same type of agony (and worse) in order to serve as your merciful high priest. He completely understands! He did all of this, in part, so that you would not have to fear death. The writer of Hebrews adds,

Since then we have a great high priest who has passed through the heavens, Jesus, the Son of God, let us hold fast our confession. For we do not have a high priest who is unable to sympathize with our weaknesses, but one who in every respect has been tempted as we are, yet without sin. Let us then with confidence draw near to the throne of grace, that we may receive mercy and find grace to help in time of need. (Heb. 4:14–16).

Jesus possesses an enormous amount of sympathy for our weaknesses. Jesus doesn't look at you with unsympathetic eyes and say, "OK, you're just consumed by sin, you need to get over yourself! You need to robotically worship me, regardless of how much pain you're in!" No, he has sympathy. He has compassion. The Bible tells us that when his friend Lazarus died, and Jesus saw the agony of Lazarus' sisters as they grieved his loss, "Jesus wept" (John 11:35). He didn't look at death and suffering with a calloused heart. No. He loves his people. He has compassion for them. He has compassion for you. His heart hurts for you when you are faced with pain and sorrow.

And when you can't pick yourself up by the bootstraps and grieve without sinning against him, or when your flesh influences you to surrender to fear or rage, do you know what Jesus is doing in those moments? Do you have any idea? He has such sympathy for you when you're being crushed under the weight of suffering, trauma, and temptation, and he loves you so much in those moments, that he mercifully goes to the throne of God *for* you! Yes, *for you!*

In Romans Paul explained it, "Who is to condemn? Christ Jesus is the one who died—more than that, who was raised—who is at the right hand of God, who indeed is interceding for us" (Rom. 8:34). Did you catch that? Jesus is interceding on your behalf. You don't know what to pray, how to pray, or have the strength to pray. Jesus has it covered! He understands the confusion and heartache this world causes, and he prays and intercedes on your behalf. His birth, life, death, resurrection, and ascension resound with eternal authority, "It is finished!" Full and glad acceptance has come, and condemnation is over for his people. Freedom has come, and the relentless dominion of sin is over for his people. He has won full salvation for them. It is done; it is over. This too is intercession for your sins and weaknesses. Amazing, isn't it? Here was Paul's response to realizing Christ's intercession for the saints: "Who shall separate us from the love of Christ? Shall tribulation, or distress, or persecution, or famine, or nakedness, or danger, or sword?" (Rom. 8:35). His answer:

> No, in all these things we are more than conquerors through him who loved us. For I am sure that neither death nor life, nor angels nor rulers, nor things present nor things to come, nor powers, nor height not depth, nor anything else in all creation, will be able to separate us from the love of God in Christ Jesus our Lord. (Rom. 8:37–39)

Paul was stunned by the faithfulness of his Savior. And do you notice his biggest concern? It isn't tribulation, distress, persecution, famine, nakedness, danger, or sword (or avoiding them at all cost). He doesn't constrict the grand story of existence down the sentences of experience. Paul isn't saying, "Your security or peace rests in your never experiencing pain again." Such a mind-set could actually exacerbate symptoms of the PTSD label.

This was not Paul's perspective or dominant concern. His main concern, the concern around which his sense of hope completely revolved, was not the eradication of potential suffering, but being separated from the love of Christ (the aspect of the grand narrative)! Those things we typically fear that wield significant power in the struggles associated with PTSD (the sentence experiences like tribulation and sword) lose their grip when understood in light of the grand narrative (being united to Christ in his eternal love). This begs the questions, Do we truly fear the right things? Do we find security in that which truly brings security? Do we place too much faith in avoiding pain? Does a guarantee of physical safety take precedence over the recognition that none of our greatest fears can separate us from God's eternal love? Has our trauma influenced us to fear things much smaller than what really counts in our eternal lives? When our thinking in this regard is jumbled, when we fail to contemplate our merciful and sympathizing Savior and the joys we have in being *eternally* united with him (whether in life or death), but we fixate instead on losing control or being harmed, we make ourselves susceptible to the symptoms associated with PTSD. When our fears are ultimately centered in the wrong things, the meaning and hope of our existence is lost. In closing, simply consider how Paul's outlook (centered in the grand narrative of God) impacted his view of death and pain:

> For the sake of Christ, then, I am content with weaknesses, insults, hardships, persecutions, and calamities. For when I am weak, then I am strong. (2 Cor. 12:10)

> Yes, and I will rejoice, for I know that through your prayers and the help of the Spirit of Jesus Christ this will turn out for my deliverance, as it is my eager expectation and hope that I will not be at all ashamed, but that with full courage now as always Christ will be honored in my body, whether by life or by death. For me to live is Christ, and to die is gain. (Phil. 1:18–21)

May Jesus grant us surpassing faith that will bring us such freedom in our circumstances!

THE HEALER OF OUR BONES

As I have expressed several times thus far, our fallen state prevents us from comprehending the totality of our existence perfectly. We see and know in part. God is well aware of this, and in his mercy has offered divine insight to help us navigate this life wisely. This is true especially in the face of suffering. God graciously makes sense of issues that to the naked eye of understanding seem senseless. He brings supernatural awareness where the eye of flesh perceives only confusion and darkness. One such place where his divine wisdom illuminates the darkness is in the issue of hardship, as the writer of Hebrews addresses for us.

> It is for discipline that you have to endure. God is treating you as sons. For what son is there whom his father does not discipline? If you are left without discipline, in which all have participated, then you are illegitimate children and not sons. Besides this, we have had earthly fathers who disciplined us and we respected them. Shall we not much more be subject to the Father of spirits and live? For they disciplined us for a short time as it seemed best to them, but he disciplines us for our good, that we may share his holiness. For the moment all discipline seems painful rather than pleasant, but later it yields the peaceful fruit of righteousness to those who have been trained by it. Therefore lift your drooping hands and strengthen your weak knees, and make straight paths for your feet, so that what is lame may not be put out of joint but rather be healed. (Heb. 12:7–13)

You may have just read this passage wondering how I could have the audacity to include it in a booklet on PTSD. You may have wondered, *Is Jeremy saying that my rape was a way God was disciplining me? Is he making the case that my being injured in a severe car accident is God's hand of discipline on my life? Is this the kind of calloused counsel he would have me believe?* There are probably counselors and pastors who have hurt people by using this passage in a heartless, compassionless sense, sending the message that all one needs to do in response to suffering is to "buck up" under God's hand of discipline. My initial response to that type of counsel is sadness, and the only adjective I have to describe it is "cruel." At the same time, we can't take the other extreme and say that this passage has no bearing on an individual who has undergone the horrors of trauma.

First, we want to recognize that the writer of Hebrews is not rebuking the reader here. Instead, he is exhorting the reader (v. 5). To rebuke a person is to reprimand him (sometimes quite sternly), but to exhort an individual is something altogether different. Exhortation is a means to encourage and inspire the person to press on! Understood properly, it is encouraging news that should provide us with the proverbial "shot in the arm" to persevere. So when we read this passage, we must first understand that the intent of the author was to encourage and inspire.

Second, discipline as understood here is not a payback or a way God is balancing the scales of your life. You can't read Hebrews here and say, "Well, God must really be angry with me because of something I've done, so he's going to punish me in order to give me the justice I deserve." To say anything remotely close to that is an extreme offense to the cross of Jesus, and it is definitely not the teaching of Christianity. If God had to pour out a single, miniscule drop of wrath upon you for any reason, then in essence he would disqualify the work of Jesus on the cross. Why? It is simple. Jesus took 100 percent of the wrath you deserve upon himself. The wrath of God for any sin you have committed or will commit has been satisfied in Christ. As a believer in Jesus, you will *never* taste the wrath of God. So when we consider the word "discipline," we cannot assume God is mad at us and pouring out difficulty so that we receive punishment for our actions. The writer of Hebrews comes from a different place.

Third, as you read this passage, it is extremely important for you to recognize the significance of the familial correlations offered by the author. He is referring to believers not as servants or followers, but as children of God! This sentiment reflects the words of John when he wrote,

> But to all who did receive him, who believed in his name, he gave the right to become children of God, who were born, not of blood nor of the will of the flesh nor of the will of man, but of God. (John 1:12–13)

You belong to God as his child, and his compassion, love, concern, mercy, and kindness toward you exceed anything you can imagine. You may reply, "Well, my dad was abusive, so when I think of God as my dad it is actually terrifying." That is understandable. However, your views of God cannot rest on your past experiences with parents. Even the best of dads would fail to give an accurate view of God as Father. He is the *perfect* Father. He never gives in when it's not in your best interest. He can't be manipulated. He won't parent you out of sinful anger. His role as *perfect* Father is revealed throughout Scripture, and it will be very important for you to study his attributes so that you can become familiar with who he actually is rather than rely on a projection of your earthly father. So, as you consider this passage, part of your task will be to understand the nature of God so that you will find hope in the One who disciplines!

What does it mean to be disciplined as children of the Most High? Most of us read Hebrews 12:7–13 and automatically ascribe God's discipline to the negative event we are experiencing. For example, if you are going through financial difficulty, you may assume the financial difficulty itself is the discipline. You've been a poor steward, so God is going to make your life miserable financially. Or, if your children are rebellious, you assume it is their rebellion that is the discipline (maybe because you were a rebellious teenager and now God is going to let you have it). In other words, God's hand of discipline is narrowed down to whatever painful or negative issue you are experiencing. This, however, is akin to the "balancing of the scales" idea I mentioned earlier. You must remember that *God did not save you to get even with you.* What an unfair dilemma that would be for you! He doesn't get satisfaction from your misery. Neither do you exist in a cosmos where karma rules the day. That is not our worldview as Christians.

Instead, discipline should be thought of through the lens of a loving, personal father shaping or transforming the heart of his child. The discipline points more to the shaping of our inner being as we respond to trial, difficulty, and, yes, even trauma, than it does the trauma itself. He will shape us with a defined objective so that we may "run with endurance the race that is set before us" (Heb. 12:1). God knows what it's going to take for us to run the race of life well, and he is committed to getting us to a place where we have the capacity to do so. How cruel he would be if he just let us flounder and failed to give us all we needed to persevere. The trauma simply provides the context for God's shaping discipline.

God's discipline occurs as he whispers his instruction into our hearts through his Word. The pain of this discipline occurs as we engage the war with sin and the flesh to follow such instruction (Heb. 12:3–4). As we bear up under the brokenness of this world with the desire to glorify him in our responses, we will need to remember that sin is absolutely opposed to God. Sin is going to influence us to resist God's ways as we walk in this fallen world. Certainly the trauma is painful; no one could deny that. But it is not the pain of trauma to which the author of Hebrews refers. Rather, it is the pain of transformation and healing as you seek obedience in the hardships of a fallen world! It is the pain of tearing your heart away from flawed physical impulses (e.g., fight or flight) or sinful desires (e.g., coveting control and safety) and walking in the path of wisdom.

The Bible tells us that when God saves us, he writes his laws and precepts upon our hearts (Jer. 31:32–34). Jesus said that if we believe in him, out of our heart will flow rivers of living water (John 7:38). If you are a Christian, God has transformed you in such a way that you now know his ways and possess longings for them. As a result you must daily engage the battle within your soul to walk in the Spirit rather than the flesh. At times this can be extremely difficult, especially in the midst of trial and hardship. It is easy to justify or rationalize sin when we have been exposed to the harshness of the fallen world. The agony of engaging this war when everything in us wants to turn and run is the pain to which the author of Hebrews refers (12:11). It is analogous to the pain we experience in training.

If you have ever lifted weights, you know that you have to do so in repetitions in order to condition your muscles. You have to lift the weight several times in a row to get the desired impact on your body (i.e., muscle growth and strength). This is called a "rep." Therefore, as you prepare to exercise, you will set a goal of, let's say, ten reps. As you begin to lift, things seem great, but by the fifth rep, your muscles begin to feel the pain of lifting and may influence a desire to quit. Your muscles scream, "STOP!" and something in you wants to throw the weight to the ground in exasperation. But, since you know your propensities so well, you wisely hire a fitness instructor to guide you through your workout. It is a good thing, because as you are tempted to give up, your fitness instructor sees your weakness and goes against your intuition and impulse. He wants you to accomplish your fitness goals. So he pushes you even harder. You want to stop, but he yells, "Give me five more; come on, you can do it!" It is a painful process, but as you engage it, the rewards of fitness will make it worth the effort.

This is what the author of Hebrews seems to be saying: view hardship as weight training to condition your soul! Being raped won't discipline you. That is not God's discipline! But how you respond to this hardship *is* his discipline (for your good). Experiencing the horrors of combat is not God's way to discipline you. If that's all discipline entailed, then the outcome would be absolutely disastrous! Discipline comes through the voice of God as he instructs you through his Word in how to effectively respond to such hardship. And what he instructs can feel painful, even impossible. However, the results of heeding God's instruction will ultimately bring peace, and, as God declares in the book of Proverbs, "Whoever listens to me will dwell secure and will be at ease, without dread of disaster" (1:33). This is the beauty and fruit of God's discipline!

Existence is endowed with suffering by its nature of being fallen. Such suffering is never outside the hand of God's sovereignty, however. If we find ourselves sitting on the floor glaring at the realities of our suffering while shaking our fist at God for being so inconsiderate as to allow those things to exist, then we will in essence find ourselves wasting our lives while our souls atrophy due to our failure to heed God's instructional discipline. Trauma or hardship is not God's way of chastisement; rather, God's discipline is revealed through his instruction to you as you are faced with such things. Your simply being subject to tragedy will not accomplish the transformation to which the author of Hebrews is referring. No, the discipline of God is guiding you and shaping you in your heart as you navigate the tragedy. This is where transformational discipline takes place. In your trial, in your trauma, in your fear or rage, God will teach you to submit to him, the Father of your spirit, so that you may live! It is here, in your heart, as you face the obstacles of life (and some of them quite severe), that God will reveal himself and his ways in order to heal you, though such healing may not always be pleasant.

What I love about the author of Hebrews as he discusses God's discipline is the fact that he is honest. He doesn't paint a fluffy picture for the believer. On the contrary he admits, "For the moment all discipline seems painful rather than pleasant, but later it yields the peaceful fruit of righteousness to those who have been trained by it" (12:11). Again, what are we being trained by? Is it the trauma or God's instruction in the midst of trauma? By now I hope you are convinced it is the latter. There is no doubt that, after a woman experiences sexual or physical abuse, learning to enter relationship without fear is a profoundly painful process. There is no question that it is extremely painful to learn to respond to a perceived threat without rage if you have served in a combat zone! Learning to walk according to the wisdom and truth of God in such circumstances can be *excruciatingly* painful, because it often requires you to walk counter to your intuition and impulses. This is exactly what the author of Hebrews tells us. It may require that we walk by faith without actual evidence of change (Heb. 11:1). If we simply follow our intuition or give in to our impulses or wait for evidence before we obey, it will only cause our hands to droop, our knees to buckle, and our joints to become dislocated.

These things will hinder our ability to run this race well. Following our own wisdom will only exacerbate the damage done by trauma. It can, if not dealt with biblically, cripple our lives. It will lead us onto paths of immense destruction. But what does the author of Hebrews recommend in such circumstances? Be trained in your pain! Be trained by the wisest, infinite Instructor the mind could ever conceive! Listen to the instruction of almighty God as he teaches you essential wisdom in navigating your traumatic path towards healing. Be trained in the wisdom of God by the transformational power of his Spirit and grace through his revealed Word. As you do, your path will be straightened, your arms will be strengthened, and your bones that were broken will be healed (Heb. 12:12–13)! It is this path and this discipline that the author promises will yield the "peaceful fruit of righteousness" (Heb. 12:11).

Principles of Perseverance

1. If you have placed faith in Jesus Christ, he is the founder of your faith and has saved you from the most horrifying trauma to which you could be subjected—hell. Do you ever wonder if he cares about you because you've had to experience tragedy? How does the fact he has given his own life to save your soul from utter darkness speak to your doubts? If he did this for you, isn't it possible that he cares deeply about those things that hurt and trouble you?

2. Journal a prayer of thanksgiving for what Jesus has done in saving you from eternal death. Read this prayer aloud to God often. If you have never placed faith in Jesus, go and visit with your pastor or a friend who is a believer in Christ. Christ beckons you to come!

3. Read Hebrews 2:14–18; 4:14–16; and Philippians 2:4–8. What do these passages say about Jesus? Why are such things important for you to remember as you seek to overcome your own pain?

4. Read Hebrews 12:7–13. What wisdom from Scripture applies to your current struggle? What does the Bible say about God's love? His sovereignty? What wisdom applies to anger, fear, bitterness, or the need for control?

5. As you seek to exercise these truths, is it painful? What does the author of Hebrews promise as you are trained by discipline? Does this provide you with any sense of hope or peace?

THE REDEMPTIVE DESTINY

By now it should be very clear that your life is a narrative that is beautifully woven within the grand and glorious meta-narrative of redemption. This narrative explains the existential reality of mankind like no other, and it offers humanity a glimpse of those things that are to come. You see, the trauma-stricken world in which we now live is only temporal, and it sets the stage for one of the most amazing experiences a believer in Jesus Christ will ever encounter. This experience will be as real as any you have ever known, and it will be so vivid that all other experiences will fade at its culmination. The author of Revelation was given a powerful vision of this event, and it is important for us to realize that this event will unfold in a real historical context in the future.

> Then I saw a new heaven and a new earth, for the first heaven and the first earth had passed away, and the sea was no more. And I saw the holy city, new Jerusalem, coming down out of heaven from God, prepared as a bride adorned for her husband. And I heard a loud voice from the throne saying, "Behold, the dwelling place of God is with man. He will dwell with them, and they will be his people, and God himself will be with them as their God. He will wipe away every tear from their eyes, and death shall be no more, neither shall there be mourning, nor crying, nor pain anymore, for the former things have passed away." And he who was seated on the throne said, "Behold, I am making all things new." (Rev. 21:1–5)

Jesus, who is the author of your faith, your sympathetic savior, and the healer of your bones, is destined to return and complete his task of making all things new. Trauma does not determine your destiny—God does! He is committed as your loving God to dwell with you and to eradicate all sorrow and death from the human experience! He will erase these horrors with the power of his loving presence! The story of redemption that is transpiring now, some of which includes seasons of immense pain, will reach a massive climax, and all that has been ravaged by the presence of sin will be restored. Your life is pointing toward this day! Our death points toward this day! We must be reminded of Paul's encouragement to the Thessalonians.

> For the Lord himself will descend from heaven with a cry of command, with the voice of an archangel, and with the sound of the trumpet of God. And the dead in Christ will rise first. Then we who are alive, who are left, will be caught up together with them in the clouds to meet the Lord in the air, and so we will always be with the Lord. Therefore encourage one another with these words. (1 Thess. 4:16–18)

These words were meant as encouragement for us! They place your existential reality into proper perspective. Death and pain are not ends to be feared, and life as we know it is not the ultimate prize to be coveted. The all-surpassing joy for the believer is that both those who have died in the faith and those who live in the faith are moving along the same time line that culminates in the return of Jesus Christ! It is in this event that the radiance of his faithfulness will brightly shine! It is in this promise of Christ's return that many believers throughout history have not only risked pain, danger, and death for his sake, but have sprinted unwaveringly into its consuming flames. Because of faith in this promise,

> some were tortured, refusing to accept release, so that they might rise again to a better life. Others suffered mocking and flogging, and even chains and imprisonment. They were stoned, they were sawn in two, they were killed with the sword. They went about in skins of sheep and goats, destitute, afflicted,

mistreated—of whom the world was not worthy—wandering about in deserts and mountains, and in dens and caves of the earth. (Heb. 11:35–38)

Right perspective cultivates divine courage! And think about this: these saints of the past suffered all these things by faith, but never saw the promise realized! The Bible says,

And all these, though commended through their faith, did not receive what was promised, since God had provided something better for us, that apart from us they should not be made perfect. (Heb. 11:39–40)

These were Old Testament believers who were looking forward in time to Christ's first coming. They had a hope in the Messiah, but never met the Messiah. God had placed them in the story at such a time when the Messiah had been promised, but had not yet come. Even so, by faith, they suffered to his eternal glory. They understood the apex of their existence rested in the hope of the coming Messiah and all he would accomplish for their lives, not in their temporal existence.

And while we face the cruelties of this world, and while the flaws of our own faith are revealed in doing so, we take comfort in the words of our Savior as we anticipate this great day.

For I have come down from heaven, not to do my own will but the will of him who sent me. And this is the will of him who sent me, that I should lose nothing of all that he has given me, but raise it up on the last day. For this is the will of my Father, that everyone who looks on the Son and believes in him should have eternal life, and I will raise him up on the last day. (John 6:38–40)

As you seek to walk the paths of brokenness often sprinkled with questions and doubt about God, the destiny of your story has been guaranteed by the faithfulness of Jesus! He will lose *none* of those that belong to him! He is committed to grasping you in his loving arms until the day he meets you face to face, at which time he will personally wipe away the tears you have cried. He will cause the terrors that have haunted you to retreat into the abyss for all eternity. He made this promise to you while on this earth and has repeatedly reminded you of this unrelenting commitment through his saints (John 10:27–29; Rom. 5:1–11; 8:14–23; 1 Peter 1:1–12)! Live your moments in light of this eternal hope so that you, like Paul, can confidently say (in the context of being afflicted, perplexed, persecuted, and struck down),

> So we do not lose heart. Though our outer self is wasting away, our inner self is being renewed day by day. For this light momentary affliction is preparing for us an eternal weight of glory beyond all comparison, as we look not to the things that are seen but to the things that are unseen. For the things that are seen are transient, but the things that are unseen are eternal. (2 Cor. 4:16–18)

May his grace give you eyes to see your momentary trauma in light of his eternal glory, and may such vision grant you peace and contentment in him! May he empower you to experience the eternal weight of glory as you understand your life in the context of the unseen and eternal (the grand narrative)—rather than limit your understanding to those things that are seen and transient (the sentences of our life).

＊

The promises you have read in this booklet are yours *if* you have placed faith in the eternal work of Jesus Christ as understood in the gospel. If you have not done so, the Lord invites all who are willing to place faith in him. It is an invitation beautifully captured in the book of Isaiah:

> Come, everyone who thirsts,
>   come to the waters;
> and he who has no money,
>   come, buy and eat!
> Come, buy wine and milk
>   without money and without price.
> Why do you spend your money for that which is not bread,
>   and your labor for that which does not satisfy?
> Listen diligently to me, and eat what is good,
>   and delight yourselves in rich food. (Is. 55:1-2)

The author of Acts put it this way: "Believe in the Lord Jesus, and you will be saved" (Acts 16:31). My prayer is that his Spirit, by his grace, will give you eyes to see and ears to hear!

MORE REDEEMING WISDOM

Throughout this booklet you have read about the importance of wisdom to your understanding. To continue to develop a divine lens through which to interpret your life, read the following from the book of Proverbs and consider how the wisdom in each applies to your traumatic experiences:

Proverbs 1:7

Proverbs 1:20–33

Proverbs 2:1–8

Proverbs 3:1–8

Proverbs 3:19–26

Proverbs 4:1–15

Proverbs 5:22–23

Proverbs 8

Proverbs 9:10–12

Proverbs 10:27–30

Proverbs 12:1

Proverbs 12:15

Proverbs 13:13

Proverbs 14:16–17

Proverbs 15:30–33

Proverbs 16:20

Proverbs 24:19–20

Proverbs 25:28

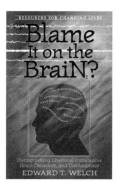

OTHER BOOKLETS IN THE GOSPEL FOR REAL LIFE SERIES

"The gospel isn't just an ethereal idea. It's not a philosophy, and it's not static. It moves and shapes and transforms the lives of those who by God's grace alone put their faith in Jesus' life, death, and resurrection. I am grateful for [the Association of Biblical Counselors]'s work of letting the gospel bear its weight on these real life sorrows and pains."
—**Matt Chandler,** lead pastor, The Village Church

ALSO IN THE SERIES:

Abuse, John Henderson

Anxiety, Robert W. Kellemen

Cutting, Jeremy Lelek

Burnout, Brad Hambrick

Depression, Margaret Ashmore

God's Attributes, Brad Hambrick

Post-Traumatic Stress Disorder, Jeremy Lelek

Sexual Abuse, Robert W. Kelleman

Vulnerability, Brad Hambrick

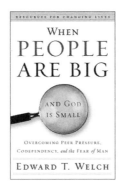

"Need people less. Love people more. That's the author's challenge. . . . He's talking about a tendency to hold other people in awe, to be controlled and mastered by them, to depend on them for what God alone can give. . . . [Welch] proposes an antidote: the fear of God . . . the believer's response to God's power, majesty and not least his mercy."
   —*Dallas Morning News*

"Refreshingly biblical . . . brimming with helpful, readable, practical insight."
   —**John MacArthur,** president of The Master's College and Seminary

"Ed Welch is a good physician of the soul. This book is enlightening, convicting, and encouraging. I highly recommend it."
   —**Jerry Bridges,** author of *Trusting God*

RESOURCES FOR CHANGING LIVES SERIES FROM P&R

Lost ambition. Emotional numbness. Fear and withdrawal. Fatigue. Marks of what is commonly called depression.

If you are one of the many people suffering from depression, there is hope and there is help—a way up when you are down. Even if you don't feel like doing anything, this booklet provides manageable steps for getting started on the path that leads out of depression.

Edward T. Welch helps us understand the spiritual issues involved, whether one's depression is caused by physical problems or results in them. Getting to the heart of what depression says and means, Welch guides us through a process of dealing with depression biblically and effectively.

OTHER BOOKLETS IN THE SERIES INCLUDE:

Anger, David Powlison
God's Love, David Powlison
Forgiveness, Robert D. Jones
Homosexuality, Edward T. Welch
Just One More, Edward T. Welch

Pornography, David Powlison
Suffering, Paul David Tripp
Suicide, Jeffrey S. Black
Thankfulness, Susan Lutz
Why Me?, David Powlison